Do Life Don't Let Life Do You!

By: C. Michele Cummings

ROYSTON
Publishing

BK Royston Publishing
Jeffersonville, IN 47131
http://www.bkroystonpublishing.com
bkroystonpublishing@gmail.com

© Copyright – 2026

All Rights Reserved. No part of this book may be reproduced, stored in a retrieval system, or transmitted by any means without the written permission of the author.

Cover Design: Elite Book Covers

ISBN-13: 978-1-967282-75-3

King James Version (KJV) – Public Domain

New International Version (NIV) - Holy Bible, New International Version®, NIV® Copyright ©1973, 1978, 1984, 2011 by Biblica, Inc.® Used by permission. All rights reserved worldwide.

Printed in the United States of America

Dedication

This book is dedicated to everyone who has ever felt overwhelmed by the challenges of life.

Table of Contents

Dedication	iii
Introduction	vii
Trusting the Process	1
Healing is Necessary	7
Worry and Confusion Can Turn to Peace	15
Uncertainty Turns to Surrender	25
Adapt	33
Prayer is the Password	45
Stretching	57
Forgiveness and Compassion	65
OK God!	73
Bag Lady	83
Adversity, Trials and Troubles	95
Complacency, Contentment, Choice	105
About the Author	117

Introduction

At times, life can be demanding and difficult to navigate. In one such moment, God spoke to me and said, "You are in this place because you have allowed it." He reminded me that everything we need has already been given to us in His Word. Scripture is our guide; it is the roadmap to life.

From this truth, the vision for this book was born. May you take time to pause, reflect on God's Word, and write what He places on your heart as you walk with Him.

Trusting the Process

Let us not fool ourselves, because we surely cannot fool God. Many behave as if they are baby Jesus. We fake and pretend to have the perfect life, knowing full well we are a complete mess. We are a complete mess we have not surrendered our life completely to the one who gave us life. In the bible in the book of Romans 10:9 a follower of Christ (Paul) tells us something. Those who confess with their mouth and believe that God raised Jesus from the dead will be saved. That is the first step, to accept God's Son, Jesus and to make him lord over your life. Some individuals stop the process here, although it proceeds beyond this stage. A process is a continued cycle with an expected end. People often feel stuck or stagnant due to personal or external factors. We are stuck on the first level. We choose what areas of our life we will allow God into, and we close the door on the others. We hope no one ever opens those doors. They hold our hidden imperfections. What is so funny about that is God has Xray vision. He knows all. It is funny to try to hide something from someone who knows everything.

My Grandmom had a saying. She said some things should stay private between you and God. Well, that is only partially true. Those are the very things that keep us in bondage. The enemy loves secrets. He uses them as leverage over you, to keep you in fear and bondage. That fear makes you do everything in your power to keep others from finding out that you have shortcomings. Confession is good for the soul. God already knows you're not perfect. He never expected you to be. You did that. Confession takes the leverage away from the enemy. Let go. Let go and let God. By surrendering your life entirely to God, shortcomings, and all you free yourself. This allows God the freedom to work in every area of your life. The process may be hard, but it will be so free and rewarding.

Nugget:

    Letting go requires a level of acceptance. Accept that you are not perfect and that is okay with God. That is right where he wants you to be at this very moment. Do not allow the enemy to have any control over you.

Let's Go Bible:

Psalm 37:5 (KJV) says "to commit your way to the Lord; trust in him, and he will act." Whatever we do, we must learn to seek God and His will for it. Once approved, the task will be done. I am not saying there will not be any hindrances along the way. Because we have committed to him, God will see us through. Trust the process.

Reflection

Reflection

Healing is Necessary

It is so necessary to take time to heal. If not, you will do like my cousin says and bleed all over the people. You spread your unresolved emotions and issues on to the next person. Unresolved trauma and hurt clouds your decision making. It can cause you to lead and advise others wrong. Simply because you are making decisions and leading people from a warped perspective.

Think about it. You can use a bandage to stop the bleeding, but you don't leave it there indefinitely. If you leave a bandage on too long, you run the risk of infection and prolong the healing. Many of us have kept the bandage on too long, and now we have an infection that we have not healed from. We all have things in our past that are unresolved.

We must at some point in time deal with them.

Take the bandage off and deal with it to keep the wound from getting infected. You must first keep that place clean and use an ointment. You must change that bandage often. It's the same way with life. Deal with that issue by first admitting there is a trauma or issue (take off the bandage).

The next step is to examine the situation closely and allow God to show you if you had any part in it. This part can be tricky. We like to blame others for our shortcomings, hurts and issues. It's hard to admit that, somehow, we may have contributed. This takes much prayer and open meditation with God. I'm not talking about blame. Be careful; many people carry around blame for someone else's actions. I'm talking about God-led self-observation. If God shows you that you contributed, repent. I heard someone say repentance comes first before forgiveness.

Ask God to forgive you and, in return, forgive yourself.

Forgiveness is a major component in healing. You don't forget the hurt. What it does is free you from a lot of unwanted emotions, stress and any other negative effects it may be having on your life. You can't fully move on and live your best life until you forgive, release and move forward. Is there a time limit on the healing process? No, there is not. You owe it to yourself to take the time to reflect and allow yourself time to heal. Guess what? Healing may mean going to a therapist. It's okay, and it doesn't make you crazy. There are people who have studied to be able to help you. Lie on that sofa! Talk it out and be healed. Sometimes, you need more than your pastor or family member. Let's be transparent. Prayer heals, but sometimes, we need a little help with that prayer. Some will not agree with that statement and it's okay. However, you do it. Just do it and be healed, so you can press toward the future and all it has for you without your past getting in your way. It's a process, and it takes time, but it is so necessary. Believe me, you will know when you have been healed. You will feel free to talk about it. There will not be restraints. It will become your testimony to help others. Believe me, when I say nothing, we go through is just for us. It is to help someone else later down the road. Go ahead and stop allowing past trauma and hurt to hinder you.

Let's face it. Life will life. Troubles will come. We can overcome trouble because Jesus said that we are overcomers. Jesus already defeated anyone or anything that trics to hold us down. Let's let go of past hurts and people who hinder us.

Let's Go Bible!

Jesus declared in John 16:33 NIV, "I have told you these things, so in me you may have peace. In this world you will have trouble. But take heart! I have overcome the world." You will find that we talk a lot about Joseph who was Jacob's son. So, I want to close this chapter speaking about him and his, shall we say, situations? Joseph endured a lot. His mother died when he was young, leaving him in the care of the very women who resented him and his mother. His own brothers sold him. His boss's wife tried to sexually assault him and lied on him. He was falsely accused and sent to jail for a crime he never committed. He was lied to and forgotten by the very one he helped. All this because he had a dream. Joseph along the way was healed and because he was healed, not only did he save an entire nation when a famine came to the land, he also saved his family. The very ones who started the ripple effects of so many issues in his life. What we see is every hardship in our life has a purpose and, in the end, it works out for our good. Romans 8:28 (KJV)

Let's do life and not allow life to do us!

Reflection

Worry and Confusion Can Turn to Peace

Can I start this chapter by being transparent? Sometimes, I worry. I am not one of those super Christians. It has always been something I have struggled with. As a matter of fact, when I was younger, I suffered with awful headaches. After seeing the doctor, he told my mom I suffered from tension headaches. So early on, I was overly concerned about everything, worried about being liked. Side note: until a couple of years ago, I thought everyone liked me (a joke). I worried about my grades, confused as to why I just couldn't make all A's. I should have accepted the fact that some A's and the rest B's was exceptional. I was confused as to why I didn't fit in with certain groups. Why was it that I couldn't do like everyone else? Why didn't the boys like me? As I got older, I worried about keeping up with the trends and being able to go on vacations. I worried about bills, sickness and not leaving others out! JUST WORRY, WORRY, and MORE WORRYING.

I spent much of my young years worried and confused. God sent two angels to help me. There were some sweet little saved ladies who would come bi-weekly to get their hair done, and every time they sat in my chair, there was a peace that I would feel. It was just so much calmness with which they spoke and even in their temperament. I will never forget, one day, the wisest of the bunch told me, 'Why worry? It changes nothing.' She also shared that I shouldn't be concerned about others not liking me or thinking I was something that I hadn't even thought I was. It was them all along. After she told me that, it was an eye opener for me. She started bringing me promise books and Bible literature. I read a devotional one day, and that scripture has been my constant reminder and my healing balm. It was Philippians 4:6-7 (NIV), 'Do not be anxious about anything, but in every situation, by prayer and petition, with thanksgiving, present your requests to God. And the peace of God which transcends all understanding, will guard your hearts and your minds in Christ Jesus.' It was entitled *Do not Worry*. That morning, it began to sink in. I thought about that peace those ladies had and how my day could be crazy, and when they would come, how they would make me feel so much better. I realized that peace came from God. It was their common denominator. They both loved and talked about God. They were my church women, as I called them. They would never beat us up for our conversations and wrongdoings. I found that they would mostly listen, and then they would always follow up with talking about something that was said in the Bible. I had gone to Sunday School as a youngster, but at this time, I was living my best life, and church wasn't in it. These ladies and their calming spirit stayed on my mind. The promise books soon turned into her bringing me Bibles and dictionaries. I was curious and I looked up that word anxious and it meant worry. From that definition, it began to sink in. Oh, my goodness. Two words jumped out at me from that scripture, worry and peace! It said if I did not worry, that regardless of my circumstances, if I prayed and was thankful, that I could ask God for help and He would give me peace. The kind of peace that would stop those tension headaches. The kind of peace that would have me not worry about what people thought of me. The kind of peace that helped me understand I was never going to be able to fit in and do some of the things the others did. And it was okay. The kind of peace that even when I'm confused about something, I can pray and wait for God to show me the answer. Because of those sweet little ladies, they have both gone on to be with the Lord now. Through their testimony and mentoring, I learned there was another way. I learned God was the key. I learned worrying does not help your situation. I have seen God turn worry to peace in my life. I have seen that when I place my concerns in God's hand, He works them out every time. God has a proven track record with me. I have tried and tried to work some things out in my own strength and it will just not work. But when I prayed, I mean really prayed and left it with God, He turned things around. I stopped worrying about relationships, financial issues and health concerns, but instead, God gave peace. I have learned, it's too hard for me, but not God! There is nothing too hard for Him. Absolutely nothing. Years of worry and confusion have turned to peace. I have learned God is powerful and has all the resources I need. I have learned to be more thankful and it has brought me more peace. You have heard it many times, but there really is always someone worse off than you. Start opening your eyes and really looking around. Thank God for all He has already done and what He will do. Lean on God and watch Him give you peace. Give it to God and trust Him. I have learned to trust God. I have traded my worry for peace.

Let's Go Bible

Joseph could have really become bitter. He was betrayed by family and lied on. He was treated by horribly by ones he loved and were supposed to love him. But I don't see in scripture where Joseph rebelled or tried to get back at others for not believing in him. The Bible says wherever Joseph was, people were drawn to him. The Bible says he found favor. I believe Joseph exhibited a peace that drew people to him. In the palace and in the jail, Joseph was calm and at peace. Again, I will say, challenges will come, and when they do, learn not to worry and trust God. He will give you peace in the midst of any circumstance. When He gives you peace, don't fret or allow others to disturb it. Remember, you are learning. You are learning that you can have peace regardless of what your circumstances looks like. Do life, don't let life do you. You already know.

Reflection

Uncertainty Turns to Surrender

There will always be times in life when we face uncertainty. Many of us have problems making decisions. We have become dependent upon others to make decisions. Maybe your parents did not think you were capable of making decisions, which caused co-dependency. Maybe it came from low self-esteem. Whether you fall in the category of being a great decision maker or lack decision making skills, it is beside the point. In this life, there will be times of uncertainty. There will be times when you are afraid to make a decision, from fear. Truth be told, we are all at some point in our lives uncertain.

May I challenge you? You learn the most in uncertain times. Take a moment and reflect. Uncertainty can surely cause dependency. God wants us to know we can depend on Him for certainty. Inside all of us, there is a still, small voice. You know, the quiet one you talk over. The one you try to drown out because you don't trust it. When you don't trust the still, small voice, you neither trust God or yourself. God equipped His creation with a helper, the Holy Spirit or Holy Ghost. She is a gift from God, to steer us in times of uncertainty. There have been times in my life when I have almost gone into a full-blown panic about making decisions and dealing with uncertainty about things working out. You may be dealing with financial difficulties, relationship issues or life in general. My experience is that when I surrendered and threw my hands up, so to speak, it all came together. In times of giving up and surrendering, God teaches us we have with us the one to depend upon to help us in times of uncertainty. Mom and Dad or your spouse may not be available in a split second when you have to make a decision, but God is.

I've learned to trust God and His moves. He knows what's already going to happen anyway. He has the inside scoop on our lives and how they work out. Surrender to the one who already knows.

We find our purpose in surrendering. For some, it's the uncertainty that holds us back. We want to be in control. The unknown and unseen can be scary, but trust God, He knows. We just have to learn to turn what we want over to what God has planned for us.

Surrender is the key to uncertainty. Surrendering to God is the act of giving up one's will and desires to God, and instead, trusting in God's plan for one's life. Surrender takes much prayer and meditation. We deal with so much uncertainty because we take on more than God intended. Therefore, we cause ourselves unnecessary worry and stress about decision making.

We have assured certainty when we learn to have faith in God. It's our way of building our relationship with God and trusting that God knows what's best for us. Lean on God. It all works out with God. The beautiful thing about God is even when we make wrong decisions, God still loves us. He allows us free choice. Believe me, it only takes making a few big, wrong choices and their repercussions; to know I need to consult

God. He is waiting and willing to help you make the choices.

Life comes with uncertainty, but God is always reliable. You can rely on Him to guide and see you through.

Let's Go Bible

Jacob and his sons were uncertain about whether they would survive the famine. But because Jacob was a God-fearing man, he heard the voice of God say, "Send your sons into Egypt, where there is help and food awaiting you and your family." Because of their uncertainty, they relied upon God for directions. This obedience leads to so many other blessings and reconciliations that we will look into.

Reflection

Reflection

Adapt

We must adapt to change.

Adapt is defined as to change or modify, to make suitable for a new purpose, situation, or environment.

Change means becoming different.

Change is inevitable. It happens whether you like it or want it to happen. Life is an ever-evolving cycle. It's like Winter, Spring, Summer and Fall. It happens, and when it does, there are some changes. Winter is cold, the plants die and wither. The Spring brings showers and time changes. Summer comes for flowers and trees to bloom. The weather is hot and so forth. In the Fall, the leaves change colors and time changes again.

Life is that way. A baby is born. They start out crawling and end up walking. Then it's time for school. They graduate, and college or work comes next. They get married and/or have children. They become grandparents. They age, and inevitably, they die. The cycle of life. Maybe not in that order, but you get it.

The problem is sometimes we don't embrace nor do we evolve with changes. When we don't, we bring unnecessary stress into our lives. We are fighting a losing battle. God is in control. We can't stop what God put in place in the beginning. God had, and still has, the master plan. It's the natural evolution of life. We are God's creation. He has an entire agenda worked out for all of His creations. His entire agenda is that we trust Him. That is what faith is. The Bible says it is impossible to please God without faith. Trust your Creator to know what is best for you. God will be with you through every process if you allow Him. You are truly never alone unless you choose to be. If you are feeling alone and hopeless right now, stop and ask Jesus to come into your life. When you do, God is with you, Holy Spirit will comfort, guide you, protect you and be your friend.

Change can be hard as we are creatures of habit. Right now, I'll bet you have a routine somewhere in your life that your family can repeat like clockwork. It could be your morning routine. I get up at 7:00 am. I shower. Get my coffee and settle in my recliner awaiting my morning word at 7:30 a.m. Around 7:50 a.m., my baby sister calls. That call ends at 8:20. I then go to my phone, read my morning devotions and post them to my social media accounts. It's now time to catch up on some morning news. I watch Good Morning America until 9:00 a.m. Then, it's off to work or starting my day soon after. We are, I say again, creatures of habit. I get really upset if that routine is disturbed too much. Don't laugh. I'm sure you can repeat a routine you have.

All of that is okay, but did you leave room for God? It could be that's God's plan for your day is something much better than what you planned. The Bible says that God has a plan for your life, to prosper you and not harm you, plans to give you hope and a future. Jeremiah 29:11 (KJV)

Listen, holding on to your past ways and the old things hinders you from receiving newness. God is always doing something new. He never changes, but the way He delivers does. He is continuously downloading new ways and ideas into His creations. When we are obedient to what He says, He blesses us and those around us.

I'm thankful for upgrades. I recently received this new, innovative, portable charger for my birthday. It is dynamic. You can charge several different things at one time, Android and iPhone. Awesome, I tell you. I was so used to having separate chargers for everything. I'd gotten upset because someone had taken my port and charger that was used for my iPad. I was upset because without the charger, I had no way to charge all these devices. Then I remembered my birthday present that my cousin gave me. She said that I could charge several different devices at once. Guess what? At this very moment, I am charging my iPad, headset and cellphone at the same time. I was fretting for nothing. God had something better. I just had to be quiet, hear the Holy Spirit speak and say there is another way that is better.

Trust Me.

Is God saying those words to you? That there is another way, a better way? Trust God. Life changes. Prime example, those children whom you evolve your entire world around grow up. Your body slows down as you age. It changes. Sickness and death will come to all of us. Marriage changes. It's about you two. It's about the kids and then, it's back to you two again. Can you handle and balance the change? Economic crisis will come and you will survive. Sometimes, you survive by changing the way you spend, think and save. Friends will come and go. And then there will be different jobs and assignments. Nothing stays the same. BUT GOD. That is why we need to trust Him through life and its cycles. Life will evolve. Some days are not so pretty, but that is when you lean the most on your unwavering friend, Jesus. Jesus loves you so much. He promised to never leave you.

I want to leave you with a few scriptures that can help while life is "lifeing."

1. Ecclesiastes 3:1 says, "To everything there is a season, and a time to every purpose under the heaven." Life has seasons.

2. 2 Corinthians 5:17 "Therefore, if anyone is in Christ, the new creation has come: the

old has gone, the new is here- God gives second chances. The old you is forgiven."

3. Romans 12:2 "Do not conform to the pattern of the world, but be transformed by the renewing of your mind. Then you will be able to test and approve what God's will is—his good, pleasing and perfect will." Ask God to renew your mind so you can see what He is doing and so you will be able to please Him.

4. Proverbs 3: 5-6 "Trust in the Lord with all your heart and lean not on your own understanding; in all your ways submit to Him, and He will make your paths straight." Trust God !!

5. Philippians 4:13 "I can do all this through Him who gives me strength." God will strengthen you.

6. Hebrews 13:5-6 "Never will I leave you; never will I forsake you." You are never alone.

7. Matthew 11:28-30 "Come to me, all you who are weary and burdened, and I will give you rest." Drop that weight. Give it to God.

8. Revelations 21:4 "He will wipe every tear from their eyes. There will be no more death or mourning or crying or pain, for the old order of things has passed away." God will wipe your tears away.

Let's Go Bible

Joseph endured change. He went from the loving arms of his mother and her death to being betrayed by his own brothers. He went to being in the palace to being put in jail and then back to the palace again. But he endu wherever life took him. Joseph trusted God to deliver him, and because of that, Joseph found God's favor. Favor followed Joseph throughout his life. The same can happen for you. Trust God through the ever-changing cycles of life.

Reflection

Reflection

Prayer is the Password

All our life, we have heard 'much prayer, much power, little prayer, little power.' That is such a true statement. There is power and purpose and treasure waiting for you, but you can only unlock it. In order to unlock it, you have to know the password, and that password is prayer!

Password is defined as a secret word or phrase that must be used to gain admission to something. In this technology-driven society, everything requires a password. Passwords unlock your secret data, phone, accounts etc. If you are like me, you forget all these passwords. But thank God. We don't need passwords for Him. Once you unlock the Kingdom, it is voice activated and mind regulated. God hears your call. It can be verbal or mind regulated. Whew. Thank you, Jesus! Meaning, God hears your thoughts also.

See there is a system that seems complicated but is simple.

1. God sent Jesus. Jesus was born of a virgin. Jesus lived and experienced life. Jesus died. Jesus rose from death. Jesus is back with His Father.
2. We must believe. Believe that Jesus did die and arose from death.
3. System identifies you (God). Now, use your password. God's password is prayer! You have unlimited access. You must use your password. It's much like your password for your accounts. The

more you use it, the easier it will be to remember.

There is so much waiting for us if we would just learn to pray. It's locked up in Heaven with our name on it. But we haven't learned to pray. We haven't learned to use our password. God's password is prayer. Every time we use it we unlock hidden blessings. We unlock things that we are unaware that we need such things like safety, provision, love, peace and joy.

Prayer is simply open communication with God. Prayer builds your relationship with God. A good relationship is built on great communication. Great communication develops trust. Trust develops faith and faith pleases God.

The Scripture says it is impossible to please God without faith. Hebrews 11:6 (KJV)

Let's go there for a moment. To please God, you must have faith. Faith is believing the unseen. God is the unseen. When you pray to the unseen God for Him to work in your life, you must believe for what you are asking for. Then God will cause those things to manifest and become reality! He rewards your trust and you seeking Him.

God is a good Father. Many do not know this because they do not pray. Unlock Heaven. Learn to pray. Seek God!

Seeking God unlocks treasures for you, rewards, shall I say. Seeking God gives clarity; seeking God has so many unlimited benefits. Prayer brings peace, especially in times of trouble. Ask Moses and the children of Israel at the Red Sea. God parted the waters. Ask Gideon, who prayed for confirmation of calling and help. God gave him the strategy to defeat his enemy. Judges 6:36-37

In this corrupt world we are living in, we need God more than ever. We need God's presence, God's glory and God's peace! You have to learn to access the kingdom! The only way is to use your password. The password is prayer. "Pray without ceasing," Paul says in 1 Thessalonians 5:17.

We have all we need. God gave us all we needed when He gave us Jesus Christ. Jesus is our savior and redeemer. He not only gave us Jesus, but the Holy Spirit, our comforter, friend and guide. Tap in and pray. We can have what we need. You have heard it before; even Jesus prayed. He prayed to our Father for what He needed here on earth while in the flesh. The disciples recorded that He would often sneek away to pray. It is recorded that on His way to Calvary, Jesus asked His disciples to sit and watch while He prayed, and they went to sleep. You need God in times of trouble; friends will let you down. Jesus was troubled about the cross. Matthew 26:39 says, "He asked God, if it is possible, may this cup be taken from me? Yet not as I will, but as You will." He prayed to God about His next move. He needed his friends but God was the only one that could help. In His uncertainty, He consulted God and surrendered to God. God is with us and He is here for us. Pray to God for confirmations. He will help you.

In times of trouble, Jesus prayed. What about you?

Even on the cross, He was still praying, this time interceding. "Father, forgive them, they know not what they are doing." Luke 23:34 (KJV). He was asking for forgiveness for the very ones who had placed Him on the cross. We are going to have to learn to do the same, pray for your enemies. Matthew 5:44 (KJV).

Pray, pray, pray. Learn to talk less to others about what is going on with you and learn to pray. Pray to the one who can fix it. He never gets tired of you calling on him. Whatever you need, He is the answer.

Let's Go Bible!

God will give you what you need. Here are a few scriptures to help you when you are praying:

Peace - Philippians 4:7 beyond understanding.

In need - 1 John 5:14-15 "Ask anything according to His will, he hears us."

Power - James 5:16 "Prayer of a righteous person is powerful and effective.

Model prayer - Matthew 6:9-13 "Our Father who art in Heaven."

Strength - 1 Chronicles 16:11 "Look to the Lord and His strength, seek His face always."

Protection - John 17:15 "Not take them out of the world but protect them from the evil one."

Alone - Psalms 145:18 "The Lord is near to all who call on Him, to all who call on Him in truth."

Request - Philippians 4:6-7 "Make your requests known to God!"

Use your password!

Marriage

Children

Coworkers

Doubt

Lack

Peace

Jesus paid the price so we could use our password: pray. You can pray about anything to your father.

The first prayer and the most important that you should learn and pray is John 9:38 (KJV). This is the sinner's prayer which is simple, Lord I believe.

Reflection

Reflection

Stretching

Stretching in the Bible, symbolizes growth, transformation, and the expansion of one's faith. It represents spiritual awakening and the pursuit of a stronger relationship with God. (<u>christianityiq.com</u>)

It means reaching deeper and expanding your understanding of God and His word.

I deal with issues with my back. I have learned that if I stretch my muscles first thing in the morning—I mean really stretch them—I'm able to operate throughout the day. Morning stretching loosens my muscles so I am more mobile during the day. Not only that, I have learned that it relaxes my mind and body, opening me up to new possibilities and new revelation every morning. It gets my blood pumping. I'm ready for the day.

Over time, our muscles tend to tighten. This causes pain and restricts our movements and motion. Well, I need us to understand that this is how our life looks when we don't stretch ourselves or when we fight against God when He stretches us. Unused muscles tighten up. So does our spiritual life and relationship with God when we are not in connection with Him. If you don't work on growing more in God, you run the risk of losing your zeal, just like those muscles. You stop operating to your capacity. The muscles work but not the same, and it can be painful. Not stretching or challenging yourself can be painful to the body and spirit.

We must learn to nurture and feed our spirit. If we are spiritually undernourished, it can cause significant damage. You stunt your growth and possibly never making it your potential and purpose intended for your life.

Life I say again is ever-changing and moving. We must do the same. God has a plan and a purpose for your life. Understand that everything has an allotted time. There are planting and preparation seasons in your life. Don't miss them by not doing the work. If God allowed a situation, it has purpose and it is a part of a larger plan He has for you. Do not fight life and its challenges. You never know what this moment could be leading up to! Believe me, I know from experience it is better to learn in the stretch because harvest is coming and you want to be prepared. Paul said these words in Philippians 3:14, "I press toward the mark, for the prize of the higher calling of God in Christ Jesus."

I want my prize, don't you? Well, let's stretch then. We grow most during challenges. Challenges and difficulties cause us to lean on God like never before. Being uncomfortable is a part of God's plan. Hang in there. The muscles have to be stretched so that you can withstand the distance. God is preparing you for your next. I want my prize, don't you? Well, let's stretch then.

Let's Go Bible

1. Joseph had to stretch beyond the fact that he was sold into slavery by his brothers. His calling in Christ was to save his family in the famine.
2. David had to press past the fact that he was overlooked when Samuel came to their home to ordain the next king. His calling in Christ was to take Saul's place as king and to open up the lineage for the Savior of the world to come.
3. Jonah had to stretch past the point that the Ninevites were sinful people. His calling was to save those sinful people by declaring a word from The Lord to them.
4. Mary had to stretch past being young and unwed. Her calling in Christ was to birth the Messiah.

5. Jesus had to stretch past the fact that He was God. His calling was to save a dying world.

Stretching is a part of this Christian journey. Sometimes, God will cause us to stretch through life circumstances. But I challenge you today to learn to press and stretch yourself more. The more you do, the more you will grow in Christ. Growing in Christ means you are getting closer to your destiny. When God sees our faith growing, He moves on our behalf. Your destiny is loading.

Reflection

Reflection

Forgiveness and Compassion

Forgiveness is a big word. It is one of the hardest things to do. We always talk about forgiving others. How often do we forgive ourselves? Remember forgiveness is for you.

Forgiveness is defined in the Bible as: God's act of pardoning sins and removing their consequences, both for individuals and between people. Condemn the fault but to spare the doer.

Human forgiveness is defined as releasing negative emotions, like resentment and bitterness towards those who have wronged us. A choice to let go of the desire for retribution.

Let's talk a little more biblically. Forgiveness is conditioned on repentance from the offender, meaning the person who wronged you, acknowledges their sin and seeks forgiveness.

Forgiveness is essential for spiritual wellbeing and can lead to emotional healing and peace.

If forgiveness leads to emotional wellbeing, no wonder so many of us are a mess. We carry around tons of unresolved guilt. Guilt can weigh heavily on your body, soul and spirit. Many of us, after repentance to God and forgiveness from God, still hold on to the guilt.

I need you to understand how God works. True repentance brings freedom, freedom in mind, soul and spirit. Unresolved quilt can weigh so heavily you will think that you are physically sick, when, really, it is a spiritual sickness. I heard my pastor say this many times and I have seen it firsthand. If you do not forgive yourself or seek God's forgiveness, you can make yourself spiritually sick. You feel bad, and you automatically think it's your body. But it's not. It's your spirit that has been contaminated so long that it has begun to affect your mind. Forgiveness is a serious thing, and unresolved issues can be the death of you.

It can show up in the body in many ways—anxiety, stress, insomnia, backaches and much more. Let me stop and say right here, I am not a medical doctor. I am just a person who has experienced and seen how forgiveness and emotions can affect the body.

In life, we will make mistakes. We will make choices and do some things we are not proud of. But God always gives us a chance and another chance and another. That chance comes through repentance. Ask God to forgive you. If you have a conscience, it will let you know when you have sinned against God and done wrong. Some people say we don't all have a conscience. I disagree. I think we choose to ignore or override it.

Listen, no one is perfect. We have all done some things we are not so proud of, which leads to my second point. Have compassion, compassion for others and yourself. Compassion is what our society has lost. Compassion is defined as sympathetic pity and concern for the sufferings or misfortunes of others. God is concerned about you. He is concerned about everything you may be going through. He is concerned about every decision you make. He is there, willing to help you and forgive you. We must learn to trust God and ask Him to forgive us even when we mess up. Trust that God does forgive and He does give another chance. Use that same concern and sympathy for others and yourself.

Many drug and alcohol addictions, suicides and even gluttony could be avoided. We use those things to fill voids and feelings of emptiness and guilt. When in actuality, we should take everything to God, allow Him to forgive us and forgive ourselves. We must trust His word that He forgives us and then we must forgive ourselves. Thirdly, please, after God has forgiven you and you have forgiven yourself, do not, and I repeat, do not allow others to keep you locked in a place of shame and guilt. The devil loves to think he has the upper hand when there are secrets and unresolved emotions and forgiveness. But remember, through The Blood of Christ Jesus, we are forgiven. We must believe that Jesus really was the Son of God and that He gave His life, His blood was shed so we could be forgiven by His Father and we could have another chance. Do not allow the enemy to hold past sins that are already forgiven by God against you. God has forgotten it so the enemy has no more power over you. Now, let's go! Who do you need to forgive?

Let's Go Bible

Luke 15:20 says, "While the son was still a long way off, his father saw him coming and felt sorry for him. So, he ran to him and hugged and kissed him."

The father forgave the son. When he saw him, and the son was headed home but not there yet, the father ran to meet him. HE FORGAVE. If that's not enough for you, Joseph forgave his brothers for selling him into slavery. Not only that, he tells them to forgive themselves. He declared that what they meant for harm, God used all for their good. God used his stay in Egypt to position him to become a leader in Egypt during a time when a great famine came over the land. Therefore, Joseph was able to save his family and others during a perilous time.

Reflection

OK God!

We are living in troubling times. Times of trouble draw us closer to God. They teach us to rely on God. Life has challenges. There will be difficulties. That is when God really shows Himself mighty. Let us be real, with all that is going on around us, if we are not careful, we may find ourselves asking God has He forgotten us. Stress, drama and confusion can cause us to lose focus. We begin focusing totally on what is going on around us and forgetting the one who has the answers.

These days can turn into weeks of nothing but sad news. If you are not careful, depression and anxiety can settle in. Followers of Christ must be extra cautious.

We are our brothers and sisters' keepers and when they hurt, we hurt. This tends to cause us to carry things we were never intended to carry. God never intended for you to do that. God is a great planner. He anticipates and knows everything we could endure. He has a solution. We must learn to seek Him for answers to every problem or concern that may present itself.

Confusion and troubling times did not just begin. It has been around for quite a while. Masking itself and distracting many from peace and fulfillment. In fact, in Paul's second letter to the Corinthians he addresses this. False prophets had infiltrated the church and had many doubting God. There was a lot of chaos and confusion happening at the time. Paul tells the church Jesus suffered and so will you. We will suffer for our convictions and beliefs. Suffering is a part of life and as Christians, we are not exempt. The good news is you are not alone in your suffering. We all have our own cross and we carry our own loads. We often try to carry our load and others. The loads become overwhelming and seem as if the pressure from it all will crush you. That is what God wants. He wants you to need Him. I hear you asking what do you mean? Our response should be "ok God.' God, I hear you and please help me to endure.

Troubles and tough times help us to learn God and to appreciate him. Are you enduring something difficult right now? Please know that God is preparing you and getting you ready for your next. You have been chosen. You are right where you need to be at this moment. Say it 'I was chosen." God chose you for this moment in this season of your life. Understand that we do not go through difficulties for ourselves. It is going to help someone else later. Think for a moment. Did you choose to be where you are right now in your life? Did you choose your job? How is motherhood? Were you really prepared to be someone's spouse? What about your financial status? How is your family? Do you love your church?

In this letter, Paul explains that being chosen means you no longer belong solely to yourself. You work for God and His will for your life. Sometimes that comes with suffering. It is a part of the calling. You are being used for a purpose. Paul has seen and endured so much. It only solidified his purpose in knowing he can manage whatever life throws at him. Paul had been beaten, shipwrecked, and left for dead. He has seen it all. God brought him through it all. God had called Paul from being a prosecutor to now being a defendant and he has purpose.

Let us understand this about God's callings. Every call is not for a pulpit. You may never hold a microphone in your hand. Your voice and the way you live before others can echo and change more lives than a microphone ever could. Some have been purposed to witness to their family. Others are called to share on their jobs. It could be that you are just to live a God-fearing life and witness in your very own home. Whichever your call is, just do it with love and humility. You have been prepared for your specific task. Oftentimes when you are being prepared for a particular occurrence God pushes you. He knows you will need a deeper experience of His power and presence. So do not allow yourself to become consumed and overwhelmed by life and its circumstances.

John said in chapter sixteen verse thirty-three that in this world you will find tribulation, distress, and suffering but be courageous, be confident, be undaunted, be filled with joy, I have overcome the world. My conquest is accomplished my victory is abiding. This is Jesus speaking. He is letting us know because He suffered and defeated death by rising from the grave that He can comfort us. Jesus can comfort us by letting us know he has overcome any situation we can face in this world. Because He overcame the difficulties of this world so can we. We have the same power living within us when we believe in Him. The power to overcome. Do not keep this to yourselves. God wants you to bring comfort to others. Let them know there are others who have gone through difficulties and come through victoriously. Let them know they are not alone. Use your afflictions to help change others. We will end like we started OK GOD. I now understand. You are only deepening my relationship with you. This is preparing me. This preparation is helping mold me for my purpose and future. OK GOD. I hear you God do life by depending on you!

Let's Go Bible

Ok God is a chapter all about accepting Gods will for your life. God has a plan for each of our lives. We do better when we accept it. God showed Joseph at an early age that his family would bow to him. Being a youngster he shared it with his family. They did not understand nor accept what joseph was telling them. He was a child sharing a dream God gave him. Often, people observe your life without truly comprehending it. Let us be honest, neither will you. I am sure Joseph could not understand how his going to jail and serving the Pharoah was beneficial to his family bowing to him. I know he could not understand how being a slave was beneficial. Joseph's life experienced a series of highs and lows. He went from the pit to the palace back to the pit and back to the palace.

It was all apart of Gods plan. Joseph must have felt much like Paul. Paul said I am content with whatever God gives me. I have developed the ability to adapt and thrive under both limited and abundant circumstances. Joseph learned early to just accept life and live it to the best of his knowledge.

The hardships and turns were preparing Joseph. God is preparing you. Wherever you are in life right now. Learn from it and just surrender by saying 'OK GOD!'

Not my will but yours be done. I surrender.

Reflection

Bag Lady

We are reminded that we can cast our cares on God because He cares for us. You can find that passage in 1 Peter 5:7. If there has ever been a time to do that, it is now. To cast means to throw. Throw all your worries and concerns on God because He can manage them.

In fishing, when you cast your net you throw it because you want that net to get as far out into the deep as possible. To cast something means to violently throw or fling something with great force. Get rid of it.

Today was a rough day for me. We all have those days when you just feel mentally and physically exhausted. Today has been that day. Lately, I just feel aggravated and agitated by the least things. Life has been wearing me out. Seems as if everything I attempt to do is just whipping me. Seemingly because life is defeating me, I am always tired. We do not do our best when we are tired. Avoid certain actions when you feel this way. First, please and I repeat please do not accept obligations that you will not be able to keep. Knowing that you have overextended yourself and are unable to keep a commitment weighs heavily on you. Second, learn balance. One task at a time. Achieve that one and then move on. Lastly be careful to offer grace when dealing with others. Juggling too much can make you irritable. We must learn it is not other people's fault that you have overcommitted. Learn to use that same grace and patience with others that you need yourself. That is a little hard to do when you are tired.

So here I am. I found myself screaming today. My plate is too full! I cannot manage it all. As I was riding along a familiar song began to play on the radio. Yes, I still listen to the radio. Erica Badu was singing Bag lady. And God spoke loud and clear.

These are the lyrics.

Bag lady you gon hurt your back.

Dragging all them bags like that

I guess nobody ever told you.

All you must hold onto

Is you, is you

One day all them bags gon get in your way

So, pack light

Pack light

One day you gon miss your bus

You cannot hurry up 'cause you got too much stuff

When they see you coming, ni#### take off running.

From you it's so true

One day he gon' say you crowding my space.

So, pack light.

    Let us stop right there. One day all them bags gon get in your way. Your back is hurting from carrying all those bags. God has a word for you.

    Jesus is saying throw the bags over to Him. Throw them before they get in your way. All those bags are blocking your view. You feel weighed down because you are carrying too much unnecessary baggage. It is in your way. It is blocking your view. Now you cannot see that help is waiting for you. Get rid of the baggage so God can show you what He really has for you. You are blocking the view of the blessings that He has for you. You have become a hoarder of baggage. You are not only carrying your bags, you have picked up others also. Let go of these bags. You are going to miss your bus and run people away because you will not let go. Get rid of that excess baggage. That stuff is holding you down. Right now, life is doing you. You are carrying too many bags. Unload all that unforgiveness, baggage from old relationships, generational mess, financial baggage, emotional baggage and get rid of those insecurities.

Cast all the unwanted and unneeded baggage onto God. He cares for you, and He wants what is best for you. What is best for you is not a bunch of old baggage from yourself and others. Jeremih 29:11 says God already knows the plans He has for you. They are plans of hope and to prosper and not to harm you. Those bags are in your way, and you cannot see what God's plans are. Get that baggage out of the way. Trust God and His plans. All you do is add unnecessary weight and confusion. Trust God and try His way.

Pack light

Everyone carries baggage. God wants us to give it to Him. Allow Him to manage it. You have allowed those things to get in your way. Free yourself from your past and other things you have been carrying around. God knows you and you are more than enough. God will free you up when you allow Him. He has a path awaiting you. Allow Him to guide you to your purpose. Stop allowing old things to get in your way. There is new waiting for you. You can have the newness of life when you take God's yoke. His yoke and load for you is much lighter. God is waiting to give you rest. Those who are burdened and weary. Cast those heavy bags and find your rest. God said He will lead you down the path of righteousness. He will refresh your soul.

Repeat this prayer. Lord, I give you, my loads. I surrender all my situations, my hurts, and my burdens to you. You can manage them better than I can. These bags are getting in my way. I cannot seem to find peace, joy, or contentment. This anxiety and these concerns for everyone and everything haunt me. I place them in your capable hands and let me never pick these bags up again. I will trust you daily for my strength and portion so I will not become overwhelmed by loads and bags again. If I happen to try to pick them up, I know the pain in my back is a reminder of what caused that pain. I do not want to feel that again.

Let's Go Bible

Jacob told his sons there is a famine in the land. Egypt is the only place with food. He told his sons to go to Egypt. Understand, Jacob's sons had sold their younger brother Joseph. They sold him and he ended up a slave in Egypt. They told their dad he was killed by animals. They were in for a surprise; he was in Egypt. He was second in command of the pharaoh and was the one they would have to ask for food. They were about to bow down to their brother.

Joseph had experienced a lot. His brothers sold him to strangers. He could have held onto bitterness and unforgiveness. He could have allowed hatred to blind him. Blind him into thinking God had left him and his dreams would never come true. Because Joseph didn't hold on to unnecessary baggage, God was able to use him and give him favor wherever he found himself. Letting go frees you up to be blessed and used by God. Joseph's dream came true; his brothers bowed to him in Egypt when they came to ask for food because of the famine. God had shown Joseph as a young man that his family would bow to him. When he shared his dream, it caused his brothers to dislike him even more. They did not like Joseph because he was his father's favorite. In all he went through he was just being prepared to be used by God for such a time as this.

Trust the process. You will understand why in a little while!

Reflection

Reflection

Adversity, Trials and Troubles

What a mouthful. Three words we hate to hear, adversity, trials and troubles.

Adversity is defined as difficulties or misfortune.

Trials are defined as tests to assess its suitability or performance.

Troubles are defined as difficulty or problems.

No one wants to hear these words. We would rather have peace, love and joy at all times. Let's face it, that is not the way life is. As a matter of fact, the Bible tells us in John 16:33 that in me (meaning Jesus) you might have peace. In the world, ye shall have tribulation: but be of good cheer; I have overcome the world. Let's break that down. If you know Jesus as your Savior, you can find peace in any situation. You can only do that because He has already overcome any obstacles that life may present. He is that Powerful. We can trust God that whatever it is, it is going to work out. Trust can be a hard thing for some of us. We want to physically see our way. That is part of the problem. God wants us to lean on Him and learn to look to Him. God will not show you everything. He wants us to have faith. Believe before we see it. Understand that troubles in life will come. The world is full of troubles. When we trust Jesus Christ we have someone working on our behalf. If you are fighting on your own, you will eventually wear yourself out. Fighting alone can cause stress, anxiety, doubt and anger to build up inside of you. Be careful when all those emotions begin to build up and control you, it causes innocent people to be injured by your actions and words.

    Life is designed to mature us. To build us up along the way. Life is an intertwined circle. We are all connected. We depend on each other. We are affected by each other. My actions affect more than me. Frustration sets in along the way when things don't go our way and it spills over. That is why we have to take the time to learn life lessons. We need to mature from them and help the next person. The only way we learn is through adversity, troubles and trials. Sad but true. Wisdom comes from life experiences good and bad. The Bible also tells us in Romans 8:28 that all things work together for good to them that love God, to them who are called according to His purpose. That's right, those failures made you stronger. If you never failed, you would never celebrate the victories. Those failures were preparing you for the success up the road. I know right now you can't possibly see how your current situation can be helping you. I promise it is. If you continue to hold on and don't give up, you will see why the trials were allowed and working for you. My Pastor Craig Myers, always says you don't know you are on the way, until something is in the way. If your experiencing adversity or obstacles, stay the course. You are on the right track. God wants your complete trust. He wants your all. God wants your completely surrendered will. He wants you to trust Him with your whole life and every part of your being.

Ultimately, troubles develop our relationship with God. Whatever you're experiencing is for your good. Two major examples, financial troubles equal reliance on God. Relationship troubles cause you to trust in God more than ever. He will never let you down. Troubles on your job they equal reliance on God. Rely on God for promotion and open doors. Some doors your education and charisma will not open. It takes God.

We were all born with a purpose and purpose is developed in adversity. Adversity is defined as difficulties and misfortune.

The Bible's definition says, God's way of getting our attention! Let's face it God would never get our attention, if we never needed Him. When things are going your way, you forget God and act like you don't need Him. It is sad to say trouble brings humility and humility breaks down resistance. Most of us have placed walls of resistance up and God has to tear those down. Only when we are humbled, can we hear God and receive His direction. Following God's direction leads to divine purpose.

I found a great illustration by P. Halsey who created the six P's of spiritual development.

1. Purpose-your divine purpose is developed in trial
2. Profitable-your trials are profitable if you submit to God and trust him.
3. Presence-God will be with you in your trials
4. Proven-faith is proven in difficulties
5. Produce - your trials will produce positive spiritual qualities in your life.

6. Perspective - a new you will emerge after this

Something good is coming from this. Trust God. Submerge yourself in prayer and meditation of God's word. He will see you through. Be careful to not become bitter in this season. Bitterness will and can hinder you. I know I hear you questioning God, why me? I am trying to do your will. The answer is simply, why not you? If Jesus suffered the cross for others, we can endure our tests, trials and tribulations. Just before elevation there is pressure. Ask David. Before he became king, he was pressured and conditioned. Before becoming President, President Obama was conditioned. Before your next, you must be conditioned and you will experience pressure. Hold on. Your next is on the way.

Let's Go Bible.

Joseph told his brothers in Genesis 50:20 you intended to harm me, but God intended it for good to accomplish what is now being done, the saving of many lives. The brothers sold Joseph because of jealousy. But God used it for Joseph's good. Joseph went through trouble after trouble. When it seemed like he was about to experience a breakthrough, something else always happened. But God. Because of his perseverance, which he learned through his troubles, he was able to withstand life and its troubles. He also allowed himself to be developed into his divine purpose. He stayed close to God and because of that he was able to discern God's word and the meaning of his dream. Which lead to his gift being used to save many lives. He was conditioned for such a time. He used wisdom and taught the people how to save so when the famine came they would be ready. He also saved the very ones who tried to destroy him. Adversity, troubles and trials are being used to condition you. Hold on, keep the faith. You are about to be elevated and used for God's glory. You are about to save lives!

Reflection

Complacency, Contentment, Choice

These three words can change your life. Funny thing is at any time in your life you can find yourself at these three crossroads. Question is, what do you want and how can they all work for your good?

First, let's define each word:

1. complacent- defined as someone who is satisfied with their own abilities or situation to the point of not feeling the need to try or change. Self-satisfaction.

2. contentment- a state of happiness and satisfaction: feeling of having everything you need. Satisfaction and ease of mind. Satisfied with one's situation in life.

3. choice- an act of selecting or making a decision when faced with two or more possibilities.

The Bible defines choice as: the power of free will bestowed upon humanity by God. Freedom to choose between good and evil, faith and doubt, obedience and rebellion. Choices affect our destiny and affect others.

Complacency in the Bible is defined as: self-satisfied state of mind that leads to a lack of vigilance, spiritual growth, or responsiveness to God's will. A lack of motivation for change or improvement.

Contentment in the Bible is defined as: an inner sense of rest and peace that comes from being right with God and knowing that He is in control of all that happens to us. It comes from trusting in God's provision and being grateful for what we have. Satisfaction with who we are, what we have, and our condition in life (compellingtruth.org). Contentment is humbly submitting to Gods will.

The Bible says some things about these stages in life. They are not to be confused. Complacency is a dangerous place to be. We are normally not alert when we are complacent. In a state of complacency, danger can sneak up on you easily.

1 Peter 5:8, Be alert and of sober mind. Your enemy the devil prowls around like a roaring lion looking for someone to devour. Complacency can destroy you. Being spiritually lukewarm allows sin to creep its way in unknowingly because you are not as alert and sober minded. Revelation 3:15-16 says, I know your deeds; you are neither cold

nor hot. How I wish you were one or the other! So, because you are lukewarm, neither hot nor cold, I am about to vomit you out my mouth. It causes an environment where sin can thrive unnoticed and unchecked. Many of us have fallen asleep in states of complacency. Because of that, sin has slipped in and fell on us. Now you find that your zeal for God is gone. The hunger is gone and we are settling. Settling because we are lukewarm. Being lukewarm is not a good place to be in God. Not only does it cause you to settle but you do not put forth the effort towards the things of God.

We don't want to be cast away by God because of our complacency and sin, instead we must do like Paul in Philippians 3:12-14, we must continue to press towards the mark of Christ Jesus. It's comfortable to be comfortable but God requires more!

God gave us choices. We can choose. We can choose to do what is right and to be obedient to God. Choosing God is never wrong and always rewarding. God created us with the freedom to make choices to live the way we want to. He doesn't Lord over us but we must choose Him as Lord. Understand that choosing God as Lord, means that you allow God to lead and have authority over you when you submit to His will. Also, there are consequences for your choices. We tend to not want to deal with the consequences and results from making bad decisions. In order to make the right choices, we must know God. Knowing God and His word is important. So many of us continue to make wrong choices, because we don't consult God about everything. God chose you and He is waiting for you to choose him. Don't allow rebellion and disobedience to cause you to make bad choices.

God gives us a way out when we are tempted to make the wrong choices. Take the escape route and stop making wrong decisions. 1 Corinthians 10:13 says, "There hath no temptation taken you but such as is common to man: but God is faithful, who will not suffer you to be tempted above that ye are able; but will with the temptation also make a way to escape, that ye may be able to bear it."

We reap what we sow. It's coming back. Choose to sow good, so you can reap good. Galatians 6:7-8 says, "Be not deceived; God is not mocked: for whatsoever a man soweth, that shall he also reap. For he that soweth to his flesh shall of the flesh reap corruption; but he that soweth to the Spirit shall of the Spirit reap life everlasting."

Be careful not to make choices based on what everyone else is doing and what is popular. The crowded ways lead to destruction, but choose the less crowded way it leads to life. Making choices can be hard. No one wants to make the hard choices but trust God to help you and know that He will never steer you wrong.

Learn to be content with God and the choices you have made. I will say it again, God will never lead you wrong. It's easy to become complacent and dodge the hard choices in life but choose God to be with you. You won't regret it. Contentment brings a satisfying peace that only God can give. Choosing God brings contentment. That contentment does not come from circumstances. Contentment comes from being rooted in Christ. We must focus on God and His kingdom. Learn not to focus on what others have or what we may want but be content and seek peace. Things don't bring contentment. In life, there will be seasons of difficulties and lack. Trust God. There will also be seasons of plenty and prosperity. In these seasons, trust God. Learn as Paul did, trust God in both ups and downs, plenty and lack. Learn that Christ gives us strength to endure in all things. So where ever you find yourself in life, whether content, complacent or having to make difficult decisions, be encouraged. God is always there and He will help you if you allow Him. Trust Him with your life. Trust Him through the good, the bad and the ugly. He promised never to leave you or forsake you. He is there. Lean on Him. Trust Him in everything. We must learn to trust God with the things He has given us. Do life and don't let life do you is all about trusting God. He's the one who gave life.

Let's Go Bible

Joseph was faced with it all. He learned the lessons in all situations, troubles, trials and tribulations that he found himself in. From these lessons, he was able to save his entire family and an entire nation. Contentment taught Joseph to choose to save during the plentiful times so that when the famine came, they were all able to sustain themselves in spite of the famine.

Reflection

Reflection

About the Author

Carolyn Michele Cummings is a proud native of Edgefield, South Carolina, where she still resides. She is the second of six children born to Cora and Charlie Cummings. A licensed cosmetologist for over 30 years, Michele has dedicated her career to helping others feel confident and beautiful inside and out. Her salon's slogan, "Where looking good is understood," reflects her passion for enhancing outer beauty while allowing inner beauty to shine. She is the owner of Salon and Barber 378 and recently expanded her entrepreneurial ventures by opening Bangs and Frills Boutique. Michele is deeply committed to serving her community. As an advocate for outreach, she believes, "We can change a nation one community at a time." She is an ordained minister and founder of C. Michele Ministries, an outreach ministry dedicated to meeting community needs. Through her Embrace and Renew sessions, she provides free monthly counseling with the help of licensed therapists who generously volunteer their services. Her ministry team, consisting of three other dynamic women, also organizes an annual Community Day a family-friendly event open to all. In her church and faith community, Michele has served in various roles, including worship leader, Sunday school teacher, and assistant to her pastor. On a broader scale, she has worked as a youth advisor and Dean of Christian Education within her district of churches.

Called to preach in 2017, Michele made history by becoming the first female pastor of her church, and the first in her district. In August 2025, she began serving as pastor of Calvary Grove Baptist Church, marking another significant milestone in her ministry journey. Above all, she describes herself as a humble servant of God, often saying, "I just want to do His will for my life."

www.ingramcontent.com/pod-product-compliance
Lightning Source LLC
Chambersburg PA
CBHW071218160426
43196CB00012B/2344